NOBLESSE OBLIGE

ANOTHER LETTER TO ANOTHER SON

BY

JAMES AGATE

HOME & VAN THAL LTD.

1944

FOR

AND ON BEHALF OF

SYD, ERN, CHARLEY

AND THEIR KIND

First Published 1944

PRINTED IN GREAT BRITAIN BY
MORRISON AND GIBB LTD., LONDON AND EDINBURGH

MY DEAR BOY,—

I want to draw your attention to a passage in the work of a great writer which I translate because I do not think that your French is quite up to it: "The immoderate taste for beauty and art leads men into monstrous excesses. In minds imbued with a frantic greed for the beautiful, all the balances of truth and justice disappear. There is a lust, a disease of the art faculties, which eats up the moral like a cancer." Had this been written by a common mind one would, of course, have attached no value to it. But it was written by a great poet and a great artist, Charles Baudelaire, whose poems you are too young to read. If you doubt my judgment ask your form-master. I think he will agree that the *Fleurs du Mal* are not the proper reading for a fourteen-year-old. Now don't misunderstand either Baudelaire or me. Neither of us is saying that art is tommy-rot. Some day, when you are older, I shall encourage you to read and see the plays of Ibsen. Among these is one called *The Wild Duck*, the point of which is that although Truth is an excellent thing, too much of it told at the wrong time to the wrong people may do irreparable harm. What Baudelaire is saying and I am echoing is that too much of art, whether it be drama, or poetry, or painting, or music, or sculpture, forced on a nation at the wrong time, may well be bad for that nation. Art is life's most exquisite decoration, but it is not the first thing in life, even for the artist. The canvases of Leonardo, the plays of Shakespeare, the symphonies of Beethoven, would be of little comfort to a man naked on a raft in mid-ocean. Let us put first things first. I admit that here and there a man may exist who would rather die than accept life on condition that he never again read a book, listened to music, or went to the theatre. I can just conceive the possibility that the man exists who, given this alternative in a draughty shed at eight o'clock in the morning and with the chaplain at his heels, would tell the smug rascal fiddling with the noose to " get on with it." Montaigne has a story of a felon who was promised a free pardon if he could find a woman to marry him. Whereupon out of the crowd a good-hearted wench stepped forward. " On with your business, good hangman," said the felon, " she limps ! " Now let me bring the matter a little nearer home. If I had to buy my life at the cost of the complete obliteration of Charles Dickens, meaning that never again would the world laugh at and with Mr. Micawber, I hope I should have the strength to reject the bargain. But hoping is as far as I will go. And I should strongly resent anybody making the decision for me. I might prefer to live a coward in my own esteem. Why, then, should I force Jones, or Smith, or Robinson, whose literary horizon is " The Greyhound," to give their lives for Art, which is something entirely beyond their ken ? For this is what the intellectuals are asking the Man in the Street to do when they insist that he shall fight their battles while they sit comfortably at home scribbling and daubing. Whereas I have every moral and spiritual authority for forcing them to give their lives in accordance with something which is within every man's ken—duty to the country which gave him birth.

I will not quarrel with the notion that art is the most exquisite thing in life. (I confess to finding it a little odd that Bacon, in all his fifty-eight essays, has not one entitled " Of Art," or whatever the Elizabethan word was.) But upon this I insist—that art can never be *more* important than, or even as important as, that life of which it is a part. Some time in the eighteenth century one Samuel Madden wrote : " Words are men's daughters, but God's sons are things." Dr. Johnson, writing about the same time, said : " I am not yet so lost in lexicography, as to forget that words are the daughters of the earth, and that things are the sons of heaven." I am not sufficiently erudite to tell you which writer cribbed from t'other. But they both meant the same thing. Let me amplify this. I remember an occasion on which that great critic and stylist Neville Cardus described the batting of Frank Woolley, the Kent cricketer who flourished before your day, in terms of Meredith's :

> Lovely are the curves of the white owl sweeping,
> Wavy in the dusk lit by one large star.

And another on which Cardus said of Woolley's off-drives that " they were like butterflies going into the flame." Now that is very pretty stuff, very lovely and very moving stuff. But it would be nonsense to pretend that it is more important than Woolley's batting. Cardus would be the first to admit that the stroke is more important than the phrase which describes it. If it were not so, then the Book of Genesis is more important than the Creation !

I have quoted a line of French poetry; now let me balance this with a line from an English poet, John Keats :

> . . . magic casements, opening on the foam
> Of perilous seas, in faery lands forlorn.

Art is something more magical, if you like, than any magic. But those who peer too intently through its casement are in this peril: they may be making fools of themselves. The peculiar peril of the artist is that he may confuse what might be with what is. You remember how, in the *Mikado*, which I took you to see during the last holidays, Ko-Ko said to the Emperor of Japan: " When Your Majesty says, ' Let a thing be done,' it's as good as done—practically, it *is* done—because Your Majesty's will is law." The artist lives in a kingdom of his own where his will is the only law. The artist says to himself: " In my world such-and-such a thing is desirable; therefore I make it happen." And goes out into the real world firmly believing that whatever he thinks desirable can be made to happen.

It is possible that, at this point, you may be asking, " What exactly do you mean by Art ? " Roughly, Art is seeing a thing in your own way. A very great critic, C. E. Montague, the man who taught me all I know about criticism, has put this better than I or anybody else can hope to do: " ' But,' it will be asked by persons justly tired of sloppy talk about art, ' what *is* an artist: what, exactly, is it in a man that makes an artist of him ? ' Well, first a proneness in his mind to revel and bask in its own sense of fact; not in the use of fact—that is for the men of affairs, the Bolingbrokes; nor in the explanation of fact—that is for the men of science; but simply in his own quick and glowing apprehension of what is about him, of all that is done on the earth or goes on in the sky, of dying and being born, of the sun, clouds, and storms, of great deeds and failures, the changes of the seasons, and the strange events of men's lives. To mix with the day's diet of sights and sounds the man of this type seems to bring a wine of his own that lights a fire in his blood as he sits at the meal. What the finest minds of other types eschew he does, and takes pains to do. To shun the dry light, to drench all he sees with himself, his own temperament, the humours of his own moods— this is not his dread but his wish, as well as his bent. ' The eye sees what the eye brings the means of seeing.' ' A fool sees not the same tree that a wise man sees.' ' You shall see the world in a grain of sand And heaven in a wild flower.' This heightened and delighted personal sense of fact, a knack of seeing visions at the instance of seen things, is the basis of art. Only the basis, though. For that art may come a man must add to it a veritable passion for arresting and defining in words, or lines and colours, or notes of music, not each or any thing that he sees, nor anybody else's sense of that thing, nor yet the greatest common measure of many trained or untrained minds' senses of it, but his own unique sense of it, the precise quality and degree of emotion that the spectacle of it breeds in him and nobody else, the net result of its contact with whatever in his own temperament he has not in common with other men. That is the truth of art, to be true less to facts without you than to yourself as stirred by facts."

" A fool sees not the same tree that a wise man sees." Exactly. You remember what I told you about Ibsen's *Wild Duck*. The same sort of trouble arises when wise men insist on forcing their wisdom upon a world of fools not ready for it, when the artist insists on ordering the world as it is by the world as he prettily imagines it.

I read every word of Sir Osbert Sitwell's *A Letter to My Son* four times, and to my dismay I found the whole of it obscured by an irony which I could not penetrate. " Whenever the crowd mentions Italians, shout ' wops ! ' ' dagos ! ' ' ice-creamers ! ' It may prove difficult for you, since you lived as a child in Italy, but you must persist." Decoding thus, I must take it to mean that in Sir Osbert's view this is the moment to proclaim to the crowd the virtues of Italian art. Perhaps I am wrong. But then Sir Osbert makes it very difficult for one to be right. Take this passage : " We live in an age of world-wide hysteria—and not without reason—when not to believe as many atrocity-stories as your neighbour believes, puts you not only in danger of hell fire, but, if he has his way, exposes you to the rigours of persecution. You would rank as a heretic, as one who refuses to place credence in the Thirty-Nine Articles, or who, by declining to take part in a witch hunt, numbers himself openly among the witches. You were even denounced the other day—for I heard it—for saying that you did not believe that in a stadium in Poland Jewish babies had been seized from their mothers' arms and used as footballs by storm-troopers. It was most injudicious of you." I cannot make out whether Sir Osbert wants us to believe or disbelieve that atrocities have been perpetrated by Nazis upon Jews.

Now I came to a sentence about which there is no possibility of misinterpretation: " It is vital to both of us that we should realise that the war is only the Great Interruption, and that your career *must* continue." I cannot think of any sentence in the English language whose implications are more pernicious. If you, my son, were of military age I would say to you: " It is vital to both of us that we should realise that the war *must* end in one way— the way of freedom, alike for nations and for individuals —that if part of the price is the interruption, or even the cutting short, of your career it will be paid." Every father has said this in his fashion to every son joining up in any branch of the Services. And every mother has said it in her fashion to every daughter. I would look you in the face and say: " Even if I knew that you, my son, were another Shakespeare, another Christopher Wren, another Elgar—I would not buy your fame at the cost of the liberty of the human spirit." And you would not want me to.

Sir Osbert holds that the artist is a man above and apart from his kind, and as such exempt from conscription. Let us examine this. Every considerable country in Europe except Great Britain insists, even though no war threatens, upon its youth undergoing military training; I know of none in which a young man would be excused because he has written a string quartet, composed an unintelligible poem, or painted a picture of three sardines swimming in a top-hat and called " Barcarolle." (The question of conscripting the mature artist does not occur, because he has done his service in his youth.) Now take war-time. I hold that in time of war a man's duty to his country comes before his duty to himself or his art. I say that in total war the individual ceases to exist except in cases where his continuing in his individualism helps the war effort. Obviously a wise Government will not put a bayonet into the hands of a William Walton, a Constant Lambert, a Clifford Curzon, a Noel Coward, a John Gielgud, or a Tommy Trinder. The point is that all artists should be willing to serve or not serve as the needs of their country demand. And to abide by the decisions made for them by a jury of conscientious and intelligent men. Did my old friend shirk his duty in the last war and plead the books that he was going to write? He did not. He continued gaily and gallantly with the Grenadier Guards.

I will not consent that these nice distinctions and exemptions shall be made just because some young man *thinks* he can compose or play or write or sing or act or dance. I maintain that the whole is greater than the part, meaning that life is more important than art. Let us suppose that it is not. Then how much of the stuff of life outside art are those who think in the Sitwellian way prepared to sacrifice in favour of the pretty bits? I see that the Soviet-Polish Commission of Inquiry has established that 600,000 victims of Nazi tyranny lie buried in Krempiecki Forest. There is no doubt that had the Russians not marched, the slaughter would still be going on. Sitwell's book invites us to imagine some Russian poet saying: "I am sorry, but you must please excuse me and my brother-poets from marching. We are artists and war is not our concern." How many new Mayakovskys and Shostakovitches does Sitwell think the Russian equivalent to our Bloomsbury would have to turn out to counterbalance that forest's 600,000 dead? Or to make up for another 600,000 lives whose loss refusal to march would undoubtedly have entailed? For myself I do not believe that the Russians are in the habit of weighing novels or musical scores against corpses.

I have in front of me a copy of the *Soviet War News* published by the Press Department of the Soviet Embassy in London for the date of August 25, 1944, and I find in it

2

an article by Boris Gorbatov, from which I cull: "Every-one, even the quietest and most unassuming Polish intellectual now has a romantic story to tell—a story that abounds in suffering and heroism. For instance, take Stanislaw Lec whom I have just met here. Before the war he was famous as a poet who combines bitter satire with a delightful playfulness. There is little playfulness in Stanislaw Lec now, but there is a great deal more bitterness. He has endured much. He worked in stone quarries and crushed the stones for road building. He spent a year in a concentration camp, in a Vernichtungs-lager, managed to escape in the uniform of an S.S. man, together with six other prisoners, then made his way to Warsaw and established contact with the underground movement. He began to publish a secret newspaper called *Soldier in the Struggle*. His underground organisa-tion was tracked down by the German police but again he managed to escape. He moved to another area and published a mimeographed newspaper called *Free People*. Later he joined the partisans in the woods and became an officer in a battalion of the People's Army. During the fighting for Lublin he hunted and disarmed fleeing Germans. I asked Stanislaw Lec: ' Are you going back to writing verse ? ' He shook his head: ' No, I am going on fighting Germans.' He has joined the Polish Army."

And if he is killed ? The loss of great or even potentially great artists is one of the horrors and the risks of war. But it is a horror which has to be faced and a risk which must be taken. " Many Men are undone by not going deep enough in Roguery, as in Gaming any Man may be a Loser who doth not play the whole Game." (I will give you Fielding's *Jonathan Wild* to read during the next holidays.) In total war nations and individuals must play the whole game.

I see in my morning paper that the Germans admit to burning another 600,000 persons at Maidenek. But for the grace of God and the valour of the Air Force, Maidenek

might have been Maidenhead. How many new Audens
and Isherwoods, Brittens and Blisses, Stanley Spencers and
Matthew Smiths would Sir Osbert deem a satisfactory
set-off for this 600,000? For even intellectuals are
thinking beings, and not even they have the nerve to say
they won't fight because they don't like fighting. Their
case has got to be: " *We won't fight because we are engaged
on work which is of greater value to the country than mere
fighting.*" Well, but what sort of work? I understand
Sir Osbert to hold that art is not life's most exquisite
decoration but " life's finest and most spiritual essence."
Yes, but finest for whom? For the few or the many?
Very well, let me divide the argument into (*a*) the few
and (*b*) the many. Taking (*a*) first, I find O. S. writing:
" A country is worth dying for, as it is worth living
for, because of the flowers its soil produces." And I
say that the SOIL ITSELF is worth living and dying for.
That, as far as I am concerned, is that. Now about (*b*).
Because Sir Osbert thinks that it would be nice if every-
body were spiritually moved by fine art he imagines
that everybody is. Never was there a greater mistake.
There are millions in this country to whom the plays of
Shakespeare, the poetry of Milton, the paintings of
Constable and the music of Delius mean less than nothing.
Now let us ask what such people are spiritually moved by.

To define the flame of ecstasy is to go back to the
first principles of all art. Shortly we may allege the
passionate quest for beauty; the search for light that
never was on sea or land; the expression of all that some
mysterious madness has taught the artist to be supremely
worth while setting down in word or paint or sound;
the effort to perpetuate beyond the grave and in terms of
his art that consciousness of the world about him which
has been said to be civilised man's " marvel and treasure."
It is the love of work brought to perfection in a garret and
on a crust. It is persistence in the face of neglect. Fame
and applause are fuel to the vanity of the artist; the flame

of ecstasy burns a spiritual oil. There is no tragedian of the Shakespearean stage, no comedian ripe with Molière and charged with character like a bursting grape, no maker of faces at the Palais-Royal who has not lighted his lamp at this serene and steady light.

Perhaps it will help to an understanding if we consider ecstasy on a humbler level. Once in a sporting paper I happened on a definition which all the thinking I have done since has not been able to better. The writer was describing a Welsh pony: " A veritable Ganymede in form, this Shooting Star has action which, when seen, makes life easier for the man who loves fine horses and fine action." Makes life easier, there's the whole secret ! The action of one little pony made life easier for this penny-a-liner, made him for the rapturous moment indifferent to ill-health, bankruptcy, death. It is the business of great art and great anything to make life easier. There is an old saying which describes people as being above themselves, and Galsworthy, in *The Silver Box*, has given his charwoman a phrase for her drunken husband—" He isn't himself." The business of great art is to raise the Ordinary Man above himself, to intoxicate him, so that he is no longer himself but is raised to a power of appreciation undreamed of in his sober senses. In this way the ecstasy in the artist speaks to the ecstasy which is in all of us. It does not do to lay down too hard and fast a rule as to what shall or shall not elevate a man above his normal self. The old Yorkshire proverb that there are trimmings for all sorts of cloth and buttons for fustian is true of the things of the spirit also. You cannot predict what will make life easier for the individual. I have been present at camp concerts where soldier-sentiment has stirred one's *heart* more than the master-pieces. I have seen an arch and fleshy singer—oh, the archness of fifty !—hold in cathedral silence a crowded music-hall notoriously profane. I have seen two plump females and a dress-coated counter-jumper, halo'd with blue, amber, and pink lights, draw with cornet, flute, and violin more tears from Godard's " Berceuse " than ever that sentimental gentleman dreamed of putting into it. Since these trumpery ballads made life easier for simple souls they have as good a right to be considered challenges to ecstasy as, in different degree, the clown twisting his apron as the curtain falls on *Sumurûn*, the negro page in *Rosenkavalier* keeping up the curtain ten seconds longer that he may pick up the dropped hand-kerchief, Samuel Butler's likening of Handel's " And the government shall be upon his shoulder " to the shoulder of the Wetterhorn, the " Holà ! holà ! que fais-tu là à la fenêtre ? " of Sarah Bernhardt in *Pelléas et Mélisande*.

Or the ecstasy may arise out of a game of golf. I remember two consecutive days on which I played first-class golf. To be more accurate, when I played golf in first-class company. The occasion was the practice days prior to some *News of the World* Tournament, and I hied me to Cassiobury with a young professional in whose golf I took a fatherly interest. He had invited me to knock round the course, and " have a look at the bunkers." Personally, I soon had my curiosity slaked. Young Walter, too, knew before the end of the round where some of them were. He had explained that he would rather play with me than a brother pro.—anything in the nature of a serious game being a mistake on the eve of a competition. He rather hoped to play badly. So I strode manfully to the tee, and with him joined the solid phalanx of champion golfers. In front of us was a four-ball—George Duncan and Abe Mitchell, Sandy Herd and Fred Leach. I watched them drive off, and then Walter said, " You go first, sir." In a voice without a quaver I instructed my caddie to make me a low tee. I was not nervous. Either you can play golf or you can't. I am one of those who can't, but can produce, on occasion, a credible counterfeit. Also my plus fours come from an irreproachable tailor, and I know all about the etiquette

of the game. That is why I waited until Mitchell had
played his second—the wee-est of chips—*and had moved
out of danger*. Then the miracle happened. I hit a peach,
long, low, and with just that suspicion of draw which
betokens your scratch player or better. Walter hit a
comparatively poor one, and then proceeded to scramble
on to the green with a No. 3 iron.

" Bung it up, sir ! " said the caddie, " it's a full shot."

The soldier who disobeys an order in battle risks only
his life; the golfer who ignores his caddie risks the hole.
I had contemplated a masterly chip, and a full shot seemed
absurd. However, I did as I was bid, and after a short
walk surveyed the result of my full mashie. My ball was
stone-dead. Furtively I looked at the quartet on the
next tee. Sandy Herd was at his eleventh waggle, Leach
was filling his pipe, Mitchell had his back to me, and
Duncan—careless fellow—was tying his bootlace. *They
had not seen my shot*. At the short fourth, 160 yards,
they invited us to go through. Walter put his ball two
yards from the pin. My precisely calculated three-
quarter iron shot, which was to be pushed into the wind,
went exactly six yards. . . .

Cassiobury was looking lovely. I do not know how
many leaves Vallombrosa boasted, but Cassiobury in
autumn is hard to excel. Not all the course had been
swept that early morning, and after driving down a lane
to delight the eye of a Poussin or a Claude one putted
through medallions of amber and russet lying as thickly
on the green as the gold pieces with which Pope Clement
offered to cover Lorraine's painting of Esther and
Ahasuerus. But golf is golf and art is art, and I feel
that to Sir Osbert the spiritual essence of life lies in the
second and not in the first.

Or the ecstasy might even be cricket. " Australia
batted first and scored 412. England—with Grace,
Ranji, Stoddart, Abel, Jackson, J. T. Brown, MacLaren,
Lilley, and Briggs to look to for runs—were all out for

231, and the Australian captain sent us in again. And once more the English cracks were reduced to littleness—all save Ranji who, in Giffen's term, 'conjured' an innings of 154 not out, out of the total of 305. Australia needed 125 for victory—a mere song on the wicket. Old Trafford gave itself up to the doldrums as soon as Iredale and Trott had comfortably made a score or so without loss. Then it was that Richardson's face was seen to be grim—his customary happy smile gone. In Australia's first innings he had bowled 68 overs for seven wickets and 168 runs. Yet he was here again, bowling like a man just born to immortal energy. And four Australian wickets were down for 45 in an hour. If only England had given the Australians a few more runs, the crowd wished out of its heart—if only Richardson could keep up his pace for another hour. But, of course, no man could expect him to bowl in this superhuman fashion for long. . . . Thus did the crowd sigh and regret. But Richardson's spirit *did* go on burning in dazzling flame. The afternoon moved slowly to the sunset—every hour an eternity. And Richardson *did* bowl and bowl and bowl, and his fury diminished not a jot. Other English bowlers faltered, but not Richardson. The fifth Australian wicket fell at 79, the sixth at 95, the seventh at 100. The Australians now wanted 25, with only three wickets in keeping, McKibbin and Jones—two rabbits—amongst them. 'Is it possible?' whispered the crowd. 'Can it be? Can we win . . . after all? . . .' Why, look at Richardson and see: England must win. This man is going to suffer no frustration. He has bowled for two hours and a half without a pause. He has bowled till Nature has pricked him with protesting pains in every nerve, in every muscle of his great frame. He has bowled till Nature can no longer make him aware that she is abused outrageously, for now he is a man in a trance, the body of him numbed and moving automatically to the only suggestion his consciousness can respond to—

' England must win, must win, must win . . .' With
nine runs still to be got, Kelly gave a chance to Lilley
at the wicket, and Lilley let the ball drop to the earth.
The heart of Richardson might have burst at this, but
it did not. To the end he strove and suffered. Australia
won by three wickets, and the players ran from the
field—all of them save Richardson. He stood at the
bowling crease, dazed. *Could* the match have been lost,
his spirit protested. Could it be that the gods had looked
on and permitted so much painful striving to go unre-
warded ? His body still shook from the violent motion.
He stood there like some fine animal baffled at the use-
lessness of great strength and effort in this world. A
companion led him to the pavilion. . . ."

This is by Neville Cardus, of course.

What is behind will-power such as Richardson showed
if it is not " spiritual essence ? " (The blindness of the
artist as a class is such that he cannot see that the spiritual
is not necessarily the æsthetic.) The match described took
place forty-eight years ago and I saw it. But I imagine
Sir Osbert will have nothing to do with cricket as part
of the spiritual essence of life. Here is his account of the
crowd at the Scarborough Cricket Festival.

" Weird women-enthusiasts, possibly the wives of the
cricketers—epicene, tweed-clad figures, crowned with
large straw-hats, wearing sensible-brown-shoes with
flapping and fantastic leather tongues lolling out of them,
and exhibiting, tucked into their coats, men's ties,
blazoned in dreadful stripes that held for them some
hidden significance—leant forward, watching with a
flushed and strained inanity, or occasionally allowed it
to be seen by a smile, glance, or exclamation, that they
had duly followed some esoteric subtlety of form or
style. The men were even less emotional. They sat
there rigidly, smoking, occasionally tapping their pipes,
as a woodpecker taps its beak, against the wooden rail in
front of them. One wondered if this was their way of

communicating with their mates, some form of expression superseded in mankind by speech. But their round, clear eyes held in them no meaning that they could possibly wish to convey to anyone. Now and again there might be a flutter of excitement at some peculiarly imbecile sally, such as when a batsman allowed himself to be caught out, or the umpire decreed, in another case, the mystic ' l.b.w.' Even the wooden contingent in the deck-chairs would then vibrate for a moment, while in the stands behind them there would be a seething of hats and handkerchiefs; but these outbursts were rare."

Yet I say that the national game has moved the Ordinary Man more than all the poets put together. I do not say that it has moved him as much as the poets have moved, to use Stevenson's phrase, " persons whose youth has been depressed by exceptionally æsthetic surroundings." I say that cricket has moved the Ordinary Man to the top of his spiritual bent, and that all infinities are equal. And so I could go on with a tale of footballers, prize-fighters, and jockeys. Where and why should I stop? To many the purr of the engine of a racing motor-car contains as much of spiritual essence as any sunset-touch, flower-bell, or chorus-ending from Euripides. My friend Jack Bergel, who was killed ferrying a plane, once told me that any perfectly running engine gave him exactly the same amount and kind of emotion as the finale to Mozart's " Jupiter." Would Sir Osbert exempt a youthful Malcolm Sargent and refuse exemption to a budding Malcolm Campbell? Given military age I should take as dim a view of the conductor who declined to serve on the strength of his rendering of " L'Après-midi d'un Faune " as I should of a racing motorist plead-ing a record of 300 miles an hour, or a cricketer hiding behind a century against the Balloon Barrage. Some find their " spiritual essence " in a star discovered, a mountain-peak scaled, a hinterland exploited, a civilisation unearthed, a disease cured, a field ploughed, a pair of boots well soled and truly heeled. Then why should we not exempt all star-gazers, climbers, archæologists, doctors, plough-men, cobblers, engineers, architects, town-planners, city surveyors, house-agents, barristers, professors, teachers, and all others who, endowed with their particular " spiritual essence," can communicate it by precept or example, each after his own kind ? If you are going to quibble with me in the clever modern way, and say that those who are not æsthetically moved cannot be spiritually minded, I would say to you this: The lout who is moved by the foot-work of some centre-forward to something above his normal emotions, who is raised by this pass or that goal the tiniest fraction above the self that he normally knows, is as much spiritually moved as the man of more complicated—I will not say finer—grain who is raised above himself by the Kreutzer Sonata. What follows ? This, my dear son: *If the artist is to be exempt from the common obligation, then every man who does for simple people what the artist does for the élite is exempt also.* I hold that neither is exempt. Your scrimshanking centre-forward would not dare to show his face in his " local " on the strength of a goal against Bolton Wanderers. I cannot see how your artist dare show himself out of uniform at the Café Royal on the strength of a canvas depicting the Power Station, Lots Road. Why should those who practise art be granted a privilege—if it be a privilege—denied to the rest of the great company of the spiritually minded ?

There is a very short poem by Walt Whitman called " The United States to Old World Critics " which I quote :

Here first the duties of to-day, the lessons of the concrete,
Wealth, order, travel, shelter, products, plenty;
As of the building of some varied, vast, perpetual edifice,
Whence to arise inevitable in time, the towering roofs, the lamps,
The solid-planted spires tall shooting to the stars.

Here Whitman states what things in the building up

of America are most important and in what sequence.
He gives them as " Wealth, order, travel, shelter, products,
plenty." No word of art, you observe: art is to come
later. In my view this should be the rule for the re-
building of all that the Nazis have destroyed. We are
to learn once again the lessons of the concrete. The
Sitwellians will not agree. Why? At this point I ask
you to read again that passage from Baudelaire which I
quoted at the beginning of this Letter: " The immoderate
taste for beauty and art leads men into monstrous excesses.
In minds imbued with a frantic greed for the beautiful,
all the balances of truth and justice disappear. There is
a lust, a disease of the art faculties, which eats up the
moral like a cancer." And, I would add, makes a mouthful
of the reasoning faculty.

And now I want a word or two about what are sometimes called the Lower Classes. I prefer that you should
call them Ordinary People. First let me say that I have
little or no belief in the power of education. I suspect
that when Lady Bracknell says: " Ignorance is like a
delicate exotic fruit—touch it, and the bloom is gone,"
Wilde means something more than a mere witticism.
In my view nine-tenths of English children are the worse
for education. And for the reason that the education they
are given is the wrong sort. " Educate " is derived from
the Latin word " educare," meaning " to lead forth."
But what is the modern system of education in this matter
of leading forth? So far as I can see, it leads the child
out of the darkness of healthy ignorance into the much
denser night of a soul-destroying commonness. I do not
believe that education in my time has had any effect
except to increase the number of ways in which the young
person of to-day can be common. You teach a young girl
to read: she peruses nothing except film magazines.
You teach her to write: at twenty she can hardly spell her
own name. You give her music lessons: her only interest
in music is the bilge vomited by crooners and dance bands.

You teach her deportment: she jitterbugs. Explore her mind and you will find nothing there except curiosity about the latest lipstick and nail-varnish. She has not learned how to speak her own language, preferring a jargon of her own. " Where was me an' Ida last night? Out Yankin'. Mine was ever such a nice boy—arst me to call 'im Texas." No one has persuaded these young women not to want to be common. The books they read, the films they see, the music they listen to— every approach to their minds is choked with commonness. And the same with the boys.

As you know, John, part of the money which enables me to keep you at school comes from the reviewing of novels and films. You once asked me what most of these novels are about. Well, here is the plot of one; and I may say that at least one of this kind appears on my desk every week. This particular novel is called *Tents of Araby* and its author is Virginia Creeper. Birdlike Joyce Merivale has married John Mainwaring because he is a colonel and has lent her father, a sporting Irish baronet, £10,000 to redeem his estates. Military duties call the colonel to pre-war Egypt, where Joyce falls under the spell of a sun-tanned Sheik with Bond-Street boots and Parisian manners. His name, among his intimates, is Rasha-Hasha-ben-Abi-ben-Dabi. One night, the husband being on lion-patrol, Rasha suggests iced coffee and sherbet perfumed with otto of roses in his palace, which he calls Abandrabandra, and which is only seventy miles away. Confused, Joyce allows herself to be driven in the Sheik's Hispano-Suiza, but is tipped the wink by the dusky chauffeur that Rasha is known as the Don Juan of the Desert and has a wife in every oasis. They arrive at the palace where Joyce, scenting her ruin if she does not avert it by a Machiavellian technique, seats herself at the magnificent Blüthstein and plays for time by running through the whole of Bach's Preludes and Fugues, all the sonatas of Beethoven and every blessed one of the

Mazurkas, Preludes, and Etudes of Chopin. She is about to start on the Diabelli Variations when Rasha, foiled in his villainous intentions, falls asleep. Joyce hears a loud snore; she flees through the olive-groves, past the hacienda, and out into the friendly Sahara where, by dint of expert running, she reaches Shepheard's Hotel, Cairo, at exactly five minutes past three. In the end Egypt declares war on China, the Colonel is accidentally shot by his batman, and it turns out that Rasha is really Henry Algernon Spender, Viscount Bray, kidnapped as a baby when his father, Joslyn de Vere, seventeenth Earl of Runnymead, was Viceroy of Madagascar. The book ends: "As Tennyson might have put it, the little town of Maidenhead had seldom seen a costlier wedding."

The nonsense I have to see on the films is wilder yet. And here is the kind of thing I must listen to every evening on the radio:

> I couldn't sleep a wink last night,
> Because we had that silly fight;
> I thought my heart would break the whole night through,
> I knew that you'd be sorry, and I'd be sorry too.
> I didn't have my favourite dream,
> The one in which I hold you tight,
> I had to call you up this morning
> To see if everything was still all right.
> Yes, I had to call you up this morning
> Because I couldn't sleep a wink last night.

This is sung in the manner of a sea-lion chewing a golosh.

My view is that Ordinary People are entitled to these idiotic novels, films, and croonings. To me the idea that a man who has been working for twelve hours on a demolition squad to make the street safe for me to walk in shall not be allowed after his bit of supper to laugh at George Formby or Arthur Askey is intellectual snobbery of the worst type. I asked the conductress of a bus the other day whether she found her

hours long. " No, not too long." " How long exactly ? "
" Five till eleven." " Do they make arrangements to get
you home ? " " Not what you might call arrangements.
Have to wait till just after midnight, and then a bus puts
me down twenty minutes from where I live. It's not too
bad, reelly," What would be too bad " reelly " would be
to prevent this valiant little soul from having her half-
hour of Bing Crosby before she starts work.

I have on my desk a letter from George, my former
chauffeur, who writes: " France is all right, but give me
the Walworth Road." And I happen to know that he
went to France willingly and would hate to return before
the job is done. I remember your telling me that last
term you did Shakespeare's *Henry V*. Well, this modern
youth who prefers the Walworth Road is, if I read his
letter aright, as fully flushed with ardour as any young
Elizabethan. It may interest you to know that I have
re-written a famous passage in Shakespeare's play for
the edification of those who think with Sir Osbert:

> We few, we happy few, we band of brothers;
> For he to-day that sheds his blood with me
> Shall be my brother; be he ne'er so vile,
> This day shall gentle his condition:
> And highbrows still in England now a-bed
> Shall think themselves accursed they were not here,
> And hold their manhoods cheap whiles any speaks
> That fought with us upon Invasion Day.

If I liked I could descant, or make a show of descanting,
upon Ronsard and Du Bellay, Molière, Racine and
Corneille, Lamartine and de Vigny, Verlaine and Rimbaud.
I think I do not lag behind anybody in my love of French
culture. But my heart goes out to the lad who wrote:
" France is all right, but give me the Walworth Road."
Let me repeat. I am a realist. I do not believe that
the cultural level of the working classes is any higher
than it was in the days of Chaucer or even Shakespeare.
I do not believe that education has the slightest effect

on them. I record in my last *Ego* having heard a young man in a bus say to his girl: " If I 'adn't seen 'im gettin' inter a fust-clawss kerridge I shouldn't never 'ave fawt 'e didn't 'ave nuffink." His girl replied: " Never mind 'im, Syd. You wasn't goin' ter take me ter the pictures Setterday, was yer ? " I gathered that the young man was on leave from the Army, and that the girl worked in a munition factory. I had no doubt that they were decent boy and girl. I felt that if they read at all they read Virginia Creeper. And I do not believe that you can ever get them to read Virginia Woolf. What is more, I do not see any point in trying, for the reason that even if you succeeded you would only attain the success that comes from scenting a Hottentot. I say that that decent, and, by cultural standards, entirely dreadful boy and girl are entitled to the pleasures proper to their kind.

Now take the Sitwellian argument that for an artist to be able to work at his best " it is necessary for him to have an endless vista of hours and days, within the space of which he can write and paint without any interruption except those which are casual or that he makes for him-self. But the modern development of ' healthy citizen-ship,' as it is called, under which every man is obliged to take a hand to repel the attacks from land, sea, and air brought upon him by his incompetence as a voter, sterilises all talent." Note the red herring of " brought upon himself by his incompetence as a voter." The main body of the passage I hold to be utter nonsense unsup-ported by the history of art. Did Rubens paint worse pictures because of his diplomatic activities ? Would *Tom Jones* have been a better novel if Fielding hadn't been a magistrate ? Would Burns have written better poetry if he had never ploughed ? Would Lamb have written better essays if he had not been employed at the East India House ? Would Walkley's criticisms have been wittier if he had not earned his living at the Post Office ?

Art is not " arty," and the people who must retire to an ivory tower before they can produce art come perilously near to being dilettante. Sir Osbert complains of the lack of encouragement given to art in this country. " Who will care for you or your fate, who will trouble to defend the cause of the young writer, painter, sculptor, musician ? And what inspiration will you be offered when theatre, ballet, concert-hall lie in ruins, and, owing to the break in training, there are no great executant artists for several decades ? " I think I never read such nonsense. I can recollect no time in the history of art in this country when more has been done, or was threatening to do, for the young artist in all branches of art. Never were there so many magazines for the encouragement of prose and verse. Never did the work of young painters find so ready a market. I understand that the complaint of impresarios is that they cannot find enough soloists and orchestral players. Recitals are happening daily at Galleries and Guildhalls. They are starting to hold classical concerts in public houses. C.E.M.A. has been founded. There is talk of giving every town its municipal theatre and every village its Dramatic Society. Even a National Theatre looms. And now for Sir Osbert's facts. At the end of five years of war a bare half-dozen or so out of London's fifty theatres has been destroyed. Only one concert hall lies in ruins, and the result has been to quintuple the audiences in a larger hall. And then I am by no means sure that encouragement is good for the arts. Take my own trade of writing. No day passes in which I do not receive the manuscript of a novel, a play, or a set of verses with a demand for my criticism. Never, in any of them, do I find a scrap of merit. Sometimes I get as many as six demands a day. I compute that in the last twenty years I must have scribbled " No Good " at the foot of some fifteen thousand MSS. Far better, in my opinion, if pen and ink and paper were made unprocurable; the really great writer would come forth even if he had to scratch his work upon the bark of trees. Greatness will out. If a man is an Edmund Kean, starvation will not stifle his flame.

A word about Sitwell's cure for German blood-lust. He writes: " Restore the League of Nations and recruit the army necessary for the enforcement of its laws from among the German people. Those who love fighting will volunteer, and, by being made to serve an ideal, and at the same time, a useful purpose, the tone of them will gradually be raised; they will feel that the future of civilisation depends on them, and will respond. The fact of being dressed in a uniform will quiet many of them. And, of course, we must see to it that they are, in the interests of the whole world, decimated every few years in border clashes and in fracas in Thibet and Central Africa. This is the sole solution that will de-totalise war : for within a generation all the Germans who would most *like* war, will have been given a taste of it, have become its victims without involving the rest of their race and the rest of the five continents." J'ever hear such bosh ? Bosh which is both infeasible and immoral. No German loves fighting for its own sake. He wants to goose-step and die in battle *for the glory of the Fatherland.* There is precious little of the kind of glory beloved of the Teuton in policing plateau and jungle. Policing, did I say ? I see very little difference between Germans " polic- ing " Thibet and Italians " policing " Abyssinia. What have the wretched Thibetans done that they must be sacrificed in order to rid Europe of an awkward problem ? Germany is Europe's first war-maker. Any League's first job must be to keep Germany in order. To do which the League is to use German soldiers. This is the very ecstasy of bosh.

And now I want to return to something I said earlier in this Letter. This is that culture is an embroidery on life and not the stuff of it. It does not follow that because a man dislikes good art and is fond of bad that he is a fool in domains outside the arts. It is my privilege to know a captain of industry whose brain controls the destinies of the greater part of a million men. He told me quite frankly that he should not worry if St. Paul's were bombed. " I should replace it with skyscrapers for the people who will be needed to put the reconstruction plans into action. Or just warehouses." The Greeks had no sense of the past and invented whatever history they wanted; for them the present and the beauty of art sufficed. My business friend slakes his spiritual thirst in the materialism of the moment, and his effort to improve upon it. He thinks that in his next incarnation he may be a cog in a machine, and hopes only that the machine will not be a cheap motor-car. He is a brilliant mathematician, a first-class bridge player, and kind to children. He adores Itma and Miss Grable's legs. He has never heard of John Gielgud. Indeed, he confided to me that he disliked the theatre because he found it too intellectual. " It can't get low enough for my taste." I remember one night during the present war overhearing a party of young American officers discussing what play they should see. They mentioned this theatre and that, arguing long and vigor- ously but without coming to any agreement. So I butted in and said: " Gentlemen, let me ask you a question. Do you want to see a drama of great spirituality and noble meaning, couched in fine nervous English, and likely to send you to your beds better men ? " " No, *sir* ! " replied the most ardent spirit. "Very well," I said, " then I recommend *Panama Hattie*." And why not ? Why must I foist on these young man that which they do not want ? I did not doubt that they were good soldiers, and I had the impression that after the war they would make good civilians.

Have patience with me, my dear boy, while I set down a few things about this Art of which Sitwell is so staunch a champion. Hogarth said that it was owing to the common sense of the English that they had not painted better. I am afraid the time is coming when it will be said of English poets that it was because they had lost their common sense that they had not poetised better. You have told me in your last letter that you want to be a poet. Here are two examples of the old and new poetry. The first was written by somebody who died more than sixty years ago:

> So have I heard the cuckoo's parting cry,
> From the wet field, through the vext garden-trees,
> Come with the volleying rain and tossing breeze:
> The bloom is gone, and with the bloom go I.

And here is a verse by a young gentleman of to-day:

> Perplexity is a blackened blasted orchard:
> The sorrowing branches are draped in serpents.
> Let us rush away
> On horses without legs
> Across hillmounds without summit.

It is of this kind of thing that Chesterton wrote: " It is no more a new school of poetry than sleeping in a ditch is a new form of architecture." You may say to me that you prefer sleeping in a ditch. I confess I have no answer to that. I do not think that the elder generation should force its views on the younger, but I hold that it should, as it were, lay the map of life and thought and art before young people, point out where the road forks and whither each fork leads. The other day, having you in mind, I bought two books which I am sending you under separate cover. The first is compiled by sixty-four young people who tell me what they think about their art and give examples of the way in which they practise it. Thus, A. holds that the speech of certain modern poets " proceeds from a point of *internal spontaneity* rather than from the *objective sensitivity* of the Socialist Realists." B., a young lady, doubts whether any period in the history of poetry has produced greater poets than Rilke, Joyce,

Yeats, D. H. Lawrence, and T. S. Eliot. C. holds that
young pear trees yearn to fling themselves over the hedge
and woo the field next door. D. is worried about black-
birds and starlings. Can it be that " the note we take for
lyric joy " is " the mad requiem of hate " ? There is a
political section in which we learn that " in order to fight
we have to degrade ourselves." The second book is a
novel about which a great deal of fuss was made at the
time of publication. The blurb, by which is meant the
puff printed by the publisher on the dust-cover, said.
" Bitter and astringent, this book should help to clear
the fog of facile progressivism and easy optimism which
blankets so many minds to-day and fatally hinders the
emergence of a new realism." Thus encouraged I set
about reading, and at first all went well. I took quite
a fancy to the burlesque hero who seemed intended for
the perfect combination of howling cad and Bloomsbury
intellectual. The fellow went bankrupt. Then " Margaret
[his wife] had the bravery to go out and find herself a
typing job at two pounds ten a week. I did nothing."
And again, " We drank hard, and everybody paid but
me." True to type, this ass wore long hair and blue
corduroy trousers. He went to musical parties where the
givers " held advanced opinions about music and thought
that Beethoven, for instance, was very dull and that
Brahms, Wagner, and Tschaikowsky were not composers
at all. They admired Duke Ellington and the less familiar
Viennese waltzes. Mozart they were still just able to
listen to. They served claret cup in bread-bins." The
war came and this flower of Percy Street welcomed the
black-out. " The absence of electric lighting revealed
new beauties in London at night, and in a night breeze
the balloon cables sang distantly and sounded, until you
had traced the sound to its source, like a music of the
spheres. The world was changing slowly but demon-
strably, and, so far as the natural senses were able to tell,
changing *not for the worse*." (Italics mine.) He wrote to

someone, " This war has come too late. I was maimed
by the last three years of peace, and do not think that I
can now be healed by a war." His contribution to the
war effort was to become a photographer of the nude.
Yes, the perfect lampoon.

And then it dawned upon me that what I had thought
to be a witty satire was intended to be taken seriously.
The author claimed to have found " a reason for choosing
out, among all mankind, those who stink unashamedly,
for consorting with lepers, thieves . . . for choosing to
be accounted scum. Scum, the rest of the world would
say. The cream, say I. The élite. . . . A man is worthless
until he has touched rock bottom. He is worth only
a little if, having once touched it, he then recoils in
anxious haste or struggles against adversity. A man
should make rock bottom his abiding-place, his nest."
I am astonished that, at the height of the greatest war in
history, paper, binding, and the labour of those who
make books should be squandered upon a philosophy
harmful, offensive, and infinitely more dangerous than
bosh.

I send you both books because that is the way I should
desire you not to write. Please note that I say " desire "
and not " command." What sort of an artist you intend
to be is your affair. As your father I am more concerned
with you as a man. I should like you to be a good man,
and I use the word " good " in something other than the
Sunday-school sense. Whether you are good in that way
or not is again your own affair. I want you to be a good
man in the sense that you pull your weight in making
the new world. And whether you do that or not is everybody's business. I have interrupted this letter for a
moment to slip a third book into your little parcel. This
is a novel called *Those Kids from Town Again*. It is by
Adrian Alington, and describes what happens when Ern
and Charley, two evacuees, go to stay with Sheila Truck,
the kind of novelist who writes books with titles like

Thatch and *Lichen*.   Here is a bit of their bedtime conversation :

>   " You don't mean to tell me, Charley," Sheila gasped, " that your father strikes your mother ? "
>   " Course 'e do, when 'e's sozzled Saturdays."
>   " How do you mean, dear—sozzled Saturdays ? " Charley sighed patiently.
>   " You ain't 'arf iggerant.   When 'e comes 'ome from the boozer."
>   " You mean your father gets drunk ? "
>   " Ar   Ain't 'arf a treat when 'e's pickled, my dad ain't."

Sheila then inquires how Charley's mother reacts, and receives the reply :

>   " Wot, Mum ?   Socks 'im back.   Don't your ma, Ern ? "

No, I don't particularly want you to write novels like Mr. Alington, even if you possessed that writer's considerable talent.   You must write your own books and choose your own subject.   What I want you to realise is that I would rather a son of mine fought for Ern and Charlie than for the young gentleman who wants to rush away on a horse without legs across hills without a summit.   And I realise perfectly that Ern and Charley are little ruffians who probably look forward to a life of alternately exercising dogs and doping them.   I wonder what Sir Osbert would make of this sentence which I have just come across in Desmond MacCarthy's article on E. M. Forster in to-day's *Sunday Times*.   " One of the themes which runs through Forster's work is that ' life in its most generous and vital aspects is not to be judged by standards of good taste.' "

Your father, my dear boy, would like, just for once, not to be misunderstood.   He does NOT say that all the young men of this country are Syds, Erns, and Charleys, and all the young women brazen little besoms interested only in hair-dyes and face-messes. He uses them to reinforce his argument that the soil of his country is as much the concern of the artist as the flowers. Sir Osbert would have your father believe that since world-wars are likely to continue the artist requires special protection. Has it not occurred to O. S. that, if all Englishmen to whom " spiritual essence " has been imparted and who can communicate it each after his kind are to sit back and look on, one of these days this country will lose one of these world-wars ? Has he considered what would be the worth of Art to a nation whose men have been either butchered or enslaved and whose women are forced to bear children to their conquerors ? But let us leave Sir Osbert in his topless ivory tower. I commend to your attention, my son, this passage which, slightly shortened, I have culled for you from Stevenson's *The Wrecker* : " I believe, if things had gone smooth with me, I should be now fallen in mind to a thing perhaps as low as many types of *bourgeois*—the implicit or exclusive artist. I have often marvelled at the impudence of gentlemen who describe and pass judgment on the life of man, in almost perfect ignorance of all its necessary elements and natural careers. Those who dwell in clubs and studios may paint excellent pictures or write enchanting novels. There is one thing they should not do : they should pass no judgment on man's destiny, for it is a thing with which they are unacquainted. Their own life is an excrescence of the moment, doomed, in the vicissitude of history, to pass and disappear. The eternal life of man, spent under sun and rain and in rude physical effort, lies upon one side, scarce changed since the beginning."

Now let me gather together the main threads of this over-long letter. They are five. ONE: There is a school of thought which maintains that great art can be produced only if the artist holds himself aloof from the crowd. I say that while some exquisite art may be produced in that way, the giant masterpieces will always bc familiar with the hum of cities and willing to lend an ear to the din of war. That interest in humanity as a whole, and not in some corner of it however precious, is the basis of all art that is entitled to be called *great*. Two: I realise that the taste of the Walworth Road is low, and I hold that ninety-five per cent. of it cannot be improved. I may be wrong, but I am putting my case at its strongest. Three: I maintain that it is the duty of the artist to fight for the Walworth Road, however low its taste, as manfully and resolutely as the Walworth Road fights for—Heaven forgive me—its betters. Four: That the greater the artist the greater the obligation. Five: Sir Osbert's policy of exemption, if carried to its logical conclusion, must result, though he may not realise it and obviously would not desire it, in the sacrifice of greater numbers of the ordinary man. And sacrifice in a lost war, since no country which exempts the best of its doers as well as thinkers can hope to prevail against a nation fighting as one man. I have no more to add except that it will be a sorry day for this country when for *Noblesse Oblige* it substitutes Art Forbids !

Your affectionate father,

London, *September* 9, 1944.